The Smart & Easy Guide To Genealogy: How To Create Your Genealogical Family Tree Using History Books, Online Tools, Ebooks, Relationships and Other Ancestry Research Techniques

Mary J. Hubert

Legal Stuff

COPYRIGHT

LIMITATION OF LIABILITY

Table of Contents

Creating Your Genealogical Tree

What you will learn by the end of this book:

• How to search for family members and create a genealogical tree

• Why heredity should be viewed as the greatest gift ever offered

• How to use computer software to research the genealogical tree

• How to discover your family's "tree"

• Where and how to research those members of your family who immigrated to America

• Where to look when searching for possible Native American ancestry

• How to differentiate truth from fiction when researching your family's history

• How to determine true and false when interviewing family members

• Why it is important to keep records of your current life for future family research

• How to arrange all information in a simple, understandable manner

- Methods of interpreting all family relationships

How to Search for Family Members and Create a Basic Tree

If you have ever felt that you don't belong or had trouble identifying yourself, you should try to research your family's history, meaning look at past generations. It can take years to search for every single member of the family, including both maternal and paternal ancestors. The process is not at all simple, and you may not find every relative, but in the end most people discover that the hard work was very rewarding.

Before starting, create a plan to use a foundation, and consider interviewing the eldest members of the family. Not only will you learn many things about your family, you also make memories that will last a lifetime when you spend time with the family elders. Make sure that you know the locations your family members have lived in, including city names and county names in addition to states. You may learn many things that it could have otherwise taken you months of research to discover.

Determine whether anyone before you has started researching your family's history. If you find someone indeed did so, you should take a look at their notes and compare with yours. Don't spend months or years on a project that has already been done for you, taking time away from further research and discovery.

One of the best starting points is to search the family house if it is available, your house, and other relatives' houses. Look for anything that could help you, such as a gift, letter, book, or other item that has been passed from one generation to the next. You may not find much, but many things can give you a starting point at least. If you have time and can do so, examine the house itself. Some may have quotes, names, or dates engraved, especially near the front porch, foundation slab, mailbox, or front path areas.

Be very careful with the things you inspect, because they are old and fragile and contain pieces of information that may be easy to miss or hard to read. Besides helping you find out the names of your relatives, possessions can give you a basic idea of their social status and their living environment. Clothing, jewelry, china, and furniture show wealth in many cases. Books provide information about their educational background. Some books may contain a dedication, marriage history, death record, or birth statistics. Jewelry items are the most likely to be engraved, such as lockets that feature photos of the owner or someone close to him or herself. The most valuable things are probably letters and photos, because they contain exact information to guide you forward in your research, including names and addresses.

Once you have examined everything available, make sure to store items in a safe place, other than traditional cardboard boxes where they could be lost, damaged, or ruined. Light damages books or letters. If the humidity is too high, some jewelry will fade, tarnish, rust, or otherwise lose color. Insects, dust and mold will also deteriorate the things stored. Before cleaning the place to be used, make sure that the substances contained in the cleaning products won't negatively affect anything. Some chemical vapors, especially when used in a closed place, give jewelry a rusty appearance. Finally, remember to handle these things with care, after all, some items may be over 100 years old and will break or fall apart easily.

Whenever possible, repair what becomes broken or damage, making sure to clean and store items carefully so that future generations can appreciate them. Remember that it was difficult for you to find all these things. Why should it be difficult for your grandchildren too? They can essentially pick it up where you left it and continue the family tradition of recording and preserving.

After searching for your family members, make a list of what you find, starting with you or your children if you have any, and go back as far as possible. Write every single thing you know about every member: their full name, date and place of birth, graduation, marriage, and/or death information, and so on. Although not everyone has grandparents and great-grandparents to interview, rely heavily on details that no one else can give because it can be very hard to verify what is found in other places.

Interviewing your family members can turn out to be a very pleasant activity. You will not only find information to create the genealogical tree, but also get to hear their life stories. When the next (or third) generation shows interest, many will open up more and maybe speak of things they have never before told. Be patient with them, especially if they experience lapses or get confused. At all times, respect them and their memories, and never pry or get angry if they are not forthcoming with every minute detail.

Heredity – The Greatest Gift Available

If you have started to create your family tree, the most useful gift you can ask for is a person's memories. Searching for ancestors' stories is not a new practice by any means, but it is once again gaining in popularity. Many people are eager to know who their ancestors were, what they did for a living, and what kinds of lives they led. If you have a family member who has begun searching for information, you could make their job easier by offering some practical gifts, such as the information you've gathered.

Family tree research software can spare anyone from spending long hours reading files in the library. This was the old research method, but now, there are plenty of software options on the market that do the exact same thing. When looking on the Internet, you will find programs that are free and others that are paid services. The payment is not exorbitant in most cases, depending on the depth of the records and comprehensive nature of storage and note-taking. These programs are easy to use even for someone who is not computer savvy.

If you come from a family that offers heraldry, or a crest, you can create a very unique and interesting gift. Many online companies reproduce coats of arms and similar family-oriented items, and they make wonderful gifts and keepsakes. Order one for yourself and hang it on the wall. Future generations will be happy to see that such a thing has been kept in the family for many years, and they are great conversation starters as well.

There are some researchers who compile stories to tell the story of a particular family, such as for biographical purposes. They usually dig very deep and they've researched many generations of records, often over hundreds of years. If you happen to be a part of those families, you are likely the find the history available for purchase in book, family tree, or chart form. It will definitely be a present that everyone enjoys.

Another great gift idea is a book containing a history of family's surnames. Every surname has a unique meaning, often describing where the family came from or something that they are known for, such as battle contributions or honesty (for instance).

When you search for information to create your family tree, you often find plenty of old and new photos. Some of them can be duplicated and some can be scanned so that future generations can enjoy them. Putting them into an album or folder is not a difficult job and doesn't cost much money (if any at all). After you've scanned them, or duplicated if desired, add references to help with identification in the future, such as the date, place, and/or persons in the photo. Put them all together in a photo album, which costs very little in most cases, and a personalized, unique present is ready. The greatest thing about offering someone a photo album is the fact that it will remain in the family, and future generations will be able to enjoy it and learn about their ancestors. Also, whenever you're visiting a relative that has a photo album, you can ask to see their photos and find new information in some cases. You can spend hours swapping stories and memories, developing relationships with even extended family members.

Photo albums and surname books are wonderful, but they are not the only things that one could offer as a family gift. Another idea is to keep a journal, of what you find, your daily life, and much more that can be passed down to the next generation. For those who love to read, a subscription to a genealogy magazine or website would be perfect. You can make it for one, two or however many years you want. If the one you want to surprise isn't very skilled when it comes to researching, but he or she is eager to learn, pay for classes in history or take them to tour a family homestead. You can also reproduce a particular picture to create a large painting that can be hung or mounted on the wall.

In times past, only family members or experts studied genealogy, but those times have passed although the process itself has changed. It is not about studying dusty old books in libraries and has become a pleasant activity for anyone who wishes to do it. If you have children, the fact that you are interested in genealogy may encourage them to be a part of reconstructing the family tree. History is not a subject the young appreciate, but if they see you enjoying it they may learn to love it.

Movies are probably the easiest way to learn. If you discover that you had relatives who fought in a specific war, you can rent a movie and watch it with the entire family. It will be both fun and educational, and you can use it as a bonding experience so long as the movie is age-appropriate. You can also watch documentaries about a certain period of time, a city, or a public persona. If you know the birthplace of your ancestors, you can learn how the place has evolved over the years.

Knowing what your relatives did for a living may help you relate to them, and you never know what you may find yourself capable of learning when you know that your family tried it and succeeded. There is a possibility that interest in historical facts evolving in your children helps them develop a lifelong love of learning and family history. Knowing more than other classmates will give them a head start in front of teachers and professors. The fact that you have introduced them to this amazing and endless world of history and genealogy will help them further their lives and will give you a sense of joy.

Learn How to Use Computer Software to Research Your Genealogical Tree

We have already discussed how tiring it can be to create your family tree, and to watch for the slightest details so as not to miss a single thing because it could make your efforts fruitless. Having only drafts in front of you may confuse you at times and this is why it is important to organize everything you find as soon as you find it. You can use tables, graphs or diagrams to put everything together, such as via chronological timelines. There are many methods of organization and clarification to choose from, including models, colors, fonts, and other ideas. Remember that they all come together in a way that will make sense to you, and do not use a categorization method that you cannot remember or decipher later. Using a chart to notate all descendants or ascendants of the family is common, or you can also make notes on each person using a chronological profile.

A pedigree chart is the simplest type of ascendant chart, which is also the basic family timeline. You are on the left side of the timeline and your box leads toward the right with other lines or boxes, each containing the name of your parents, grandparents, great-grandparents, and so on. You can work with four generations or up to fourteen or more, but most people start with about four to six generations of ancestors and extended family members. It is easiest to work with four in the beginning, because you have room for all of them in one chart. For the older sets of relatives, you can use a separate chart and notate the genealogical connection.

In a pedigree chart, you usually put only the most important information, without mentioning the source. Start by noting the name, including any surnames or maiden names when available, then add the place and date of birth as well as place and date of death when possible. Other things to include are major life-changing events, such as a divorce or marriage. Make sure to keep comprehensive notes when you have them, store them separately from the pedigree chart, so that you have a more accurate and complete history for your records later. In time, you can add more information to the chart or remove some if you discover they were not accurate or more is learned.

Usually, when completing a pedigree chart you will see that every member of the family gets two entries. In the first one, he or she is mentioned as being the son of two other family members. In the other one, his or her life as a spouse and a parent is displayed. Either way, each sheet contains information on a couple, traditionally a married couple although not always the case, such as their time and birth place, educational institution from which they graduated, marriage(s), places where they worked or apprenticed, other names used (especially women), birth/death places for their children, and so on.

When creating detailed records, mention the source where you have found the information, such as family Bibles, word of mouth, Internet, and so on. In case of a misunderstanding, it can easily be checked and it provides a reference point for you and others when necessary.

A descendant chart is a little more complicated to complete. First, you will need an ascendant chart and individual charts as a foundation or reference. The first name that appears on the chart is the one of your first ancestor, the oldest matriarch or patriarch known to the family. His or her descendants are next, and it comes forward to the youngest family of the member, which can be you, your children, or even your grandchildren. You can choose to include direct descendants only, leading to you/them, or put many details, such as aunts, uncles, cousins, step-families, and so forth.

A chronological profile is used to record in detail the life of a single member of the family. It can be someone you are really interested in or it can be you, depending on what you are creating. You may want your future relatives to know more about your lifestyle and save them the overwhelming work you are going through to recreate the genealogical tree, using it as an addition to a current family tree.

When creating a chronological profile, divide the information into events and draw vertical columns to separate one event from another. In each column, write a detailed description of the event, the date when it happened, and the age of the person. The basic things to include are birthplace and birthdate, the person's spouse, age and date of the marriage, the location and date of death, christenings or births of children, graduations, jobs or apprenticeships, change of homeplace or country, the implication in any political party, court hearings, war service period, and similar details.

Creating a chronological profile gives you an opportunity to search for even those in-depth details, giving you access to family secrets that you might not otherwise find (both positive and negative family information). You may discover that some information was wrong or mixed up. The most commonly discovered errors are marriages or births, graduation or military service, retirement age, and other odd facts. You should either determine whether the source you have used is correct or if it was your fact-taking that was faulty. When reading a chronological profile, you may learn that you had many things, even everything, wrong about that particular individual's life. Work hard to find the right or missing information and correct the mistake.

Research Family Members Who Immigrated To America

Centuries ago in many cases, some ancestor made the choice to come to the "Land of Opportunity". This is how America began to grow and expand as a country, eventually becoming the melting pot she is today. In the beginning, they came to explore the new land, and over the years, this reason faded and was replaced with other reasons. Immigrants chose America whenever their country was ravaged by war, when looking for a place to start a new life, or hoping to find a new, better home. Some of them came to America to study at one of the most prestigious colleges in the world, or to learn a trade to support themselves and their families. Thousands came to America to work and earn money to send home to their not-so-fortunate families, especially during the World Wars, to avoid living under harsh dictatorships or other cruel regimes.

When creating a genealogical tree, you may have some difficulty finding family members who emigrated. They arrived in the States in such great numbers that it might take quite some time to find accurate records of their arrival. The list of immigrants is not endless, although it may feel that way in the beginning, so eventually you will get what you want in many cases.

If you search for family members who immigrated to America before 1820, you should know that not only were the records poorly documented, but the number of immigrants was over ten thousand people, leading to many typographical errors. After this year, it became a little more difficult to enter America, more detailed information was required, and therefore records are more complete.

Up to 1870, so many people were arriving in America that it became absolutely essential to introduce additional laws. If you are looking for family members who came to America after 1920, it becomes far easier due to changes in regulations, meaning that all immigrants were far more carefully recorded. Their arrival was always thoroughly noted, and from that point forward it becomes nearly impossible to lose records of arrival.

When you feel that you've found all you can find on your own, remember that you can go online and find several companies that track down any family member who immigrated to America. An approximate date on which a family member arrived is helpful, but the companies can often work with nothing more than names and basic date of birth information. If you do not want to spend hours (even years) poring over old Immigration and Naturalization records, they can do it for you, for a fairly hefty price in most cases.

Ship registries are great sources of information, such as by checking records linked to Ellis Island, New York arrivals. The name you are looking for would be on the passengers' list, and you may learn of spouses, children, and other information previously unknown. It will save you a lot of time if you know an approximate date or/and the port of arrival. The trick is to find those who provide passenger manifests for free, such as a website, but some will charge a small fee for this service. You can use the Internet to look for lists but sometimes libraries are most helpful because they keep so many records.

It is a very taxing job to search for family members and recreate your genealogical tree, so do not be afraid to ask for help from your family. You may have other family members interested in history who would be happy to give you a hand. With so much information to go through, it is possible—and very likely—to miss some things. If no close family member is interested in helping you, plenty of genealogy bulletin boards are on the Internet with extended family members. All you have to do is post a query and wait for others to respond or post in a genealogy magazine. Some are willing to offer help in order to discover new information for their own genealogical trees.

If you don't want to go through the entire process of searching for family members, you can look at indices that have already been created. One of the most valuable genealogical libraries in the world is the LDS (Latter Day Saints) Family Search Center. You can find hundreds of family trees already compiled. Otherwise, it might become unavoidable to pay to research information from other sources.

Searching For Native American Ancestors

The first place to visit when you decide to follow leads in your Native American ancestry is the Bureau of Indian Affairs, also known as the BIA. It was created in 1824 as a part of the War Department and its main purpose was to recruit tribes to fight during times of war. They also made — and helped break — treaties with various tribes and white settlers.

When you contact the Bureau of Indian Affairs, they will inform you that they have no knowledge of any recording or databases. They will soon admit that there are some locations around the country in possession of some research information about Indian ancestry, but there is no list or database. When you call them, make sure you have exact information about the person you believe is/was Native American. The tribe the person belonged to is an absolute must, as well as the full name and birth date. If you do not have this information, they will not be able to provide you with any details or proof. Some branches of the Bureau claim that they do not have records, but they have rolls – current records of lists, or can direct you to them.

The Bureau of Indian Affairs took a census every year for many years. You can always look through their records, so long as that particular year has not been destroyed by a natural disaster. If you know the name of the tribe it is very helpful, because censuses were taken and sorted by tribal affiliation. Before 1930, the census contained the person's name, including whether it was the birth name in English, Native American, or both. The age, year, and place of birth are also written, as well as what the person's relationship was with other member of the house, tribe, and so on. Each person was given a roll number. Starting in 1930, every census also contained the marital status and the address of the residence, but most important was the person's percentage (estimated or known) of Native American blood. This last tidbit helps you discover your Native American bloodline faster.

If you don't know anyone who can help you read the censuses, it can be a little challenging. The first thing to know is that in order to search for the one you need, you must have a clue about the region the person you are looking for came from, and the less information you have, the more difficult the task becomes in most cases. Knowing some basic information narrows your work tremendously. Below you will find a list of tribes and some contact information, but if you don't find the one you are looking for, libraries usually keep current records of them in great detail.

If the Bureau of Indian Affairs refuses to give you any information, or simply claims that they have no records to offer, feel free to contact local offices that record Indian archives. They are more likely to help you, and they can also give you more information than the Bureau of Indian Affairs.

American Indian Center
4115 Connecticut Street St. Louis, MO 63116
(314) 773 - 3316

Bureau of Indian Affairs Muskogee Agency
4th Floor Federal Bldg. Muskogee OK 74401

Cherokee National Historical Society and Cherokee
Registration Office
P. O. Box 515 Tahlequah, OK 74464 - 0515
(918) 456 - 6007

Chief, Archives Branch Federal Archives and Records Center
P. O. Box 6216 Fort Worth, TX 76115

(Delaware, Osage, Shawnee and Kaw tribes) Kansas State
Historical Society
120 West Tenth Topeka, KS 66612 - 1291

Heart of America Indian Center
1340 E. Admiral Boulevard Kansas City MO, 64124
(816) 421 - 7608, Fax (816) 421 - 6493

LDS Library
35 North West Temple Street, Salt Lake City, UT 84150

Newberry Library
60 West Walton Street Chicago, IL 60610 - 3394

Northern Cherokee Nation of the Old Louisiana Territory
1012 Business Highway 63 North Columbia, MO 65201
(573) 44 3 -8424

Saponi Nation of Missouri Mahenips Band
c/o 3445 CR 4990 Willow Springs, MO, 65793
(417) 469 - 2547

Southwest Missouri Indian Center
2422 W. Division Springfield, MO 65802

(417) 869 - 9550, Fax (417) 869 - 0922

The Oklahoma Historical Society
2100 N. Lincoln Oklahoma City, OK 73105

Differentiating Truth from Fiction When Searching Your Family's History

Creating your genealogical tree is a long-term, overwhelming process without having to factor in time for any mistakes. The most important thing is to be sure of the sources you are using: the information you get must be true and reliable. Looking through so many records and files, you will find a huge amount of information, but not all of it is accurate. Some will mislead you and cause you to spend hours, weeks, sometimes even months or years on the wrong track. You have to differentiate what is true from what is false, but there are methods of separating facts from falsehoods.

There are two types of evidence — direct and indirect — to know if you are on the right track with your research. First, you must identify the type of information you are using. Direct evidence represents clear information that you don't have to check or recheck in order to verify. Direct evidence will perfectly complete other information that you have found. The people and places are clear, the timeline matches, and you don't need any kind of verification. Indirect evidence represents unclear and incomplete information that must be verified to determine veracity or it may lead you on a record wild goose chase. You will have to put more effort into seeing if it is true and whether it fits your family history, often more effort than it is worth.

The primary sources to use when creating your genealogical tree are verifiable records of all types: marriage, birth, baptism, burials, military services, and so on. These offer real, provable facts. When you discover a fact you don't know very much about, check one of the records to see if it is true and can be used in your genealogy. Compare the information you have with information from the records. Those count as your primary source. From this point on, since you have created a solid foundation, you can start searching for information from additional, less easily verified sources, such as magazines, websites, or genealogy newspapers.

Remember that you must always check the source you are using if you want your research to be true. Otherwise, in the end you may find yourself having to start from scratch since too much information is missing or inaccurate. Magazines or newspapers may publish things just for the sake of it without having any thought for facts. You must choose only articles that have some type of reputation for veracity, and avoid tabloid-type sources. This applies to websites, also; look for records written around the exact moment an event took place since these usually contain the most reliable information. That information will lead you to other verifiable sources almost every time.

Records that were made after an event took place may contain errors or missing/incomplete information. These are called secondary sources. If you use them, you must ascertain whether they offer reliable information. This is another waste of time in many cases, but a necessary one because it is impossible to find all of the information you need just by reading primary sources.

All sources should offer a guarantee that the information is true. Any reference that you find when you read a source must be able to pass a verification test. You should find it where it says you can find it. If you can't find it, the information is false and the references are not genuine sources. When it comes to websites, it is easier to verify because they usually offer direct links as references.

After you verify the information, you can start to put it all together and create the branches of the genealogical tree. This is where you will discover gaps in your research and you can proceed to check other sources. While reading other sources, you may find some information that contradicts some facts that you thought were true, so be sure to double check those and do your best to correct missing or incorrect data.

True and False Information When Interviewing Family Members

When you begin to interview family members, especially the older ones, you should be prepared to hear all kinds of stories. Some of them may be true; some of them may not. Ask the person you are interviewing how they know about a certain fact, and check different sources to ensure credibility. Some stories may contain both a true fact and a false tidbit, so it is important to learn to separate and differentiate between the two.

Every family builds its history on myths mixed with grains of truth, and most members of the family take pride in being part of a mystical fact whether it is completely true or partly false. For example, your grandmother may tell you that her grandmother descended from a long line of Indian princesses. This is a common myth you may encounter if your line goes back to a Cherokee tribe. An Indian princess can also be known as a Navajo or Apache princess. The fact evolved because of preconceived notions that have no real foundation in Native American tribes, ruled by chiefs or medicine men and rarely recording anything that would have been worded to read "princess".

Native Americans had real trouble accepting marriages between a white male and a woman of their type and vice versa. It can be difficult to trace these bloodlines in some cases, so be sure that all "facts" about the family can be verified on paper. Another thing to remember is that if you know you come from a line of Native Americans, there is a small chance that this is not true. There was a time when saying you carry the Native American ancestry was very popular and meant access to government money, and so many people claimed it, although they were not actually Native Americans.

Immigration stories are very common, such as your grandmother telling you that her grandfather emigrated with his five brothers. This may not be accurate, and it may have been four brothers, two brothers and a sister, or no family members at all. Double check all word of mouth sources. Another well-told myth is that of the stowaway immigrant. These myths lend an aura of mysticism to your family's history, so don't be surprised if you get a few of these stories, and keep in mind that they are probably wild goose chases. Your Indian princess ancestress who was a stowaway wouldn't have been recorded on any registry as such in almost all ship registries, but rather just listed at the end of that particular passenger list with everyone else.

Your grandparent may brag about you being related to someone famous—or infamous—that he saw on TV or read about and admired very much. Just because you share a name with a celebrity, icon, or outlaw doesn't mean you are relatives. There are few situations where people come from the same line as someone famous/infamous. Chances are good that you are no relation, but you should still double check, because there is always that small chance that the stories are true.

Probably one of the most common myths is the idea that a person's surname was changed at Ellis Island, New York during immigration and naturalization. Ellis Island was known as the Gateway of Immigrants, but few if any names were ever changed there. Some of them were compared with the list that was made when the ship sailed just to make sure, and, if some names were changed, it was only because some immigrants wanted to fit in better with American society, not because the officials of the port wanted the name changed. More common that name changes were misspellings, often due to poor communication or dictation during that era.

Because there are so many myths that need to be verified, the safest way to discover new information is to read as many sources as possible. The idea that something is written down gives you a sense of security. It is easier to interview family members because spending time with them represents a few hours of joy, just keep in mind that most families are ordinary and don't have a famous or mystical background. So although telling stories that are not true about the family line may give some people a feeling of great importance, make sure you run the story by other family members that are not as likely to misrepresent the truth or forget key elements. If you can't use a documented source, ask for help from your older relatives.

Understanding Why It Is Important To Keep Records of Your Current Life for the Future

When you decide to create your genealogy tree, eventually you will have to start writing. You can't realistically just gather information and throw it all in a box. You want to write the document as if it were a book, using an easy-to-read style so all members of the family, including the little ones and the adults, can understand and enjoy it.

When you start writing, remember that all information must be documented. Just because you are not going to publish it doesn't mean that the sources you used shouldn't be documented for future reference. One of the reasons is that documentation can help you in your efforts. It is obvious that you will not be spending twenty hours searching for sources every single day. You probably have a job, and obviously a family, so creating a genealogical tree will be a hobby. You will need to pick everything up from where you left it a month before, or whenever you were last able to work on the material. References will help you continue writing as if you'd just stopped a minute ago. Also, if you need to look up something again after you have written it, you can utilize the references.

You researchers can help other people who decide to build their research from yours. Documenting your sources can prevent others from going through the exact process of elimination and verification that you did. Your documentation will help the one doing further research on your documentation know what sources you used. If you write your document basing it on others' research, it will save you time also.

Future generations are more likely to trust your research if you provide evidence. Even convincing your immediate family that your research contains only the facts requires the use of verifiable documentation. Not a single world you write should be considered a joke or a myth. In the future, you may find yourself thinking about publishing your research so that others can either learn how to create a family tree or to show relatives with whom you have no contact about your mutual family. For this, you sometimes need a professional researcher. He or will also check the veracity and your documentation will be a real help.

You shouldn't worry that the process of documenting is a difficult one. In fact, it is actually very simple and it doesn't take much time in many cases. When you were in school, you may or may not have liked to document things. We all remember how difficult it was to put together a biography. It is true that the documentation must follow a format, but it is easy to understand if you pay attention and keep up with organization from the beginning. For instance, say that you found your great-grandmother's name on an official census. You don't have to record all of the routes that brought you to that specific census, but the name of it, where it was recorded, and the page where you found the name should be mentioned. When you document a census, make sure that you get right the roll number and the page number as well. Every family has a number, too.

Sample entry: James, Mary, John, Martha, Elizabeth, and June Smith 1895 entries, U.S. Official Census Record (State of Kansas), Page 21-22, Lines 47-50.

This is, of course, a basic format you can use. You can write down more information, if there is enough space. Also, if you intend to publish your research, it is recommended that you stick to a specific format for the duration of the project. That way, everyone will understand it in the future. The order should be: author, title of the article, name of the publication that contains the article (including edition number if applicable), where it was published, who published it, year it was published, and page numbers. Using this basic format, you can list up to three authors. If more than three authors wrote the article, notate only the name of the first author and add "et al" to the entry.

If your source is an anthology, notate both the title of the book and the title of the article. Put the title of the article in quotation marks and italicize the book title.

Probably the most important information within the entry is the publisher information. One publishing house usually has more than one location where it does business. Similar books may be published at the same time, and it can become confusing to learn which house actually published a particular book. Additionally, not all publishing houses are still operational, some have since closed, bankrupted, sold out, or merged with others. This prevents you from locating a specific publisher.

The last information the entry contains is the page number(s). It probably took some time to look through all of those pages, and you don't want to repeat the process or doom others to do so. Mentioning the page number simplifies the job for further researchers. They (or you) can read your documentation and go straight to the page number that you notated.

Learn To Make Information Easy To Understand For Future Family Researchers

Keep records of what you have learned, even if it doesn't pan out very far, so that future researchers can pick up the scent when more information comes to light. What is the point of reading so many censuses, magazines, and newspapers, or interviewing family members, if you don't record it? It will benefit you as well as future family members. If they are looking for a specific fact they can always come and look for it in your research. Recording the information gives others the possibility to learn about their family and stop believing that they came from a long line of Indian princesses.

You can't work without taking breaks. Some of them may be longer than others, say a week or a month. When you record your progress, you know exactly where to pick things up when you start the work again.

The fact that you record your research gives others the feeling that whatever you are writing must be true. Some of them may be more inclined to give you a hand with your research when they see that it is legit. You can ask those who help you to look for other sources and compare them with your information. The more sources you use the more errors you will find and have the chance to fix. Information that is verified by two people is more likely to be correct than that done by one lone researcher.

Future members of the family who show interest in genealogy will probably verify your research. In your research, there may be gaps you found impossible to fill. Providing recorders with information gives a chance for your future family to look through it again and compare information they find in order to complete the genealogical tree. New information can always be added later, and old information modified. You may be the one who started researching, but your children's children may continue it and pass it to future generations. As I said, it is a hobby that your entire line could learn to enjoy.

Seeing you so passionate with what you are doing, your children may ask you to let them help. You have made them interested in history and genealogy. In the beginning, give them simple tasks to perform. As they learn, they can look for new sources themselves. If they want to continue the research on their own, the fact that you provided them a solid foundation will save them money, energy, and time. You gave them a direction and they can follow it. This is a great reason to record everything you read, every person you talk to, every place you go; to help others continue your research without having to recheck the information you provided.

If you believe that time will change people so much that they will show no interest in history or their family line, you shouldn't stop recording the research. There is at least one future family member who will be interested in reading your work. Recording also helps you for further researchers, even decades down the road. Let's say that you find some new information about your great-grandfather that is completely different from what you thought. Records allow you to backtrack and discover what fact is true, the old one or the new.

If you have forgotten some information, the fact that you keep records of every single step will come in handy. It will be easier to locate the information in your records than to try to find it again later.

You can use a computer to organize all of this information. Charts and tables will make it easier to access. You can also make it visible to other people who use the Internet to start or continue their own searches.

How to Arrange Information in a Simple, Understandable Manner

As you create your genealogical tree, follow the steps written below to streamline the process and make it easier to organize:

1. Collect what you need before you start.

Materials needed include: boxes with lids, multicolored hanging file folders, standard green hanging file folders, manila folders, all sorts of pens and highlighters, labels for folders, Post-it notes, star stickers, lined paper, blank paper, a wall size pedigree chart (purchase at the library or online on ancestry websites). Extra boxes to store all of the files can also come in handy for sure. It is important to store all of your materials and research in a safe place, such as a craft room or office, and although a garage sounds perfect, make sure there are no dangerous openings that allow wind, dust, or humidity to come inside and ruin the boxes.

2. Categorize the family pedigree charts.

Use a printer to print each of the pedigree charts. Store them in a green hanging folder labeled "Pedigree Charts". Come back any time that you find some new information that you want to add to one of the charts. Keep some blank sheets in the folder just in case you need them.

3. Use the circled five-generation Pedigree Charts.

Print a copy of the Pedigree Chart. The first generation dates way back to your sixteenth great-grandmother. Now, the fifth generation is you. The Chart is classified with a color code. It is a common Chart, so if you go online, you will find it on many different genealogy websites. Prices will vary based on where you purchase, but computer-savvy researchers may be able to create their own without much difficulty.

4. Each box should contain sixteen hanging file folders.

Because you have sixteen great-grandparents, you will need sixteen files. Place them into a box. As time goes by, you may need to add more, but sixteen is the basic number that should start each one.

5. Every colored hanging file folder should contain a family surname.

You have eight great-grandfathers and eight great-grandmothers. Each folder should have the names of your grandfathers and the maiden names of all of your grandmothers. It may be a little difficult to find maiden names for some of your great-grandmothers, but it is necessary in order to trace the ancestry accurately.

6. In each colored folder, there should be a copy of the five-generation pedigree chart.

Print another sixteen copies of the chart. Highlight them before putting them in the folders. The highlight color is based on the last name of the relatives in that folder, using a pedigree chart to categorize each highlighted color and last name combination. Each color-coded pedigree chart goes into the last name hanging folder that it designates.

7. Your five-generation pedigree chart should contain files for each family.

Apply colored labels to each file tab, using separate manila folders for each individual family surname. Make sure the color you use is the same as the color used for group records, using colored labels or Post-it notes that can easily be moved or changed. This allows you to place another label over the existing one in case you have written something wrong or need to modify it later.

8. File the manila folders.

Place your manila folders into the hanging file folders. Again, be sure that the color of the label for the manila folders is the same as the color of the hanging file folder. The colors make everything so much easier and more efficient.

9. Every family folder must contain recordings, documents.

All verified family information must be kept inside the folder. No item should be forgotten or set aside for "later" placement, or it could easily be lost.

In separate files with appropriate labels, add photos, birth certificates, death certificates, letters and other correspondence, pieces of newspapers, pages of diaries, and so on. These sorts of things will be of some use at some point during your research. Add those files to the appropriate hanging file for the person/family they are connected with. For instance, add the folder labeled "Pictures of Mary Smith children" to the file where "Mary Smith" may be found.

In summary, you will constantly be adding to your collection, so do not be surprised when its dimensions change and you need to move transfer things into a bigger box. Each box should contain things related to one category. Just remember that if you don't keep the boxes organized, it will make things difficult to find when needed.

Interpreting Relationships for Your Family

This genealogy hobby can be both really exciting and almost overwhelming. Looking through so many registers takes a lot of time and dedication. Once you discover that a person is related to you somehow, you have to search for more to learn the type of relationship. In the world of genealogy, you will find plenty of terms to label the relationships between relatives. It may get confusing at times but few people have trouble understanding the basic terms.

There are quite a few labels and terms when it comes to cousins and these are often the most confusing. It is difficult to comprehend when your mother tells you a guy is your fourth cousin, three times removed. Put simply, "cousins" have the same grandparents, great-grandparents, and so on. Your first cousins are the children of your aunts and uncles. Your second cousins don't have common grandparents, but they share a common great-grandparent.

Your children and the children of your first cousins are considered second cousins. It goes on the same for third, fourth, fifth cousins and on. Third cousins have the same great-great-grandparents, fourth cousins have the same great-great-great-grandparents, and etc. It is a little difficult to go back far enough with your research to find your fifth cousins. You share the same great-great-great-great-grandparents, so you really have to dig a lot to find them.

Now, what does "removed cousins" indicate? It definitely evokes mental images of divorce and/or deportation, but uncommon occurrences centuries ago. Two removed cousins simply means that they are not from the same generation. If a cousin is once removed, it means one generation of difference. Twice removed would indicate two generations of difference, and so on. For example: Your father's first cousin is your first cousin, once removed.

It is hard enough for you to understand this relationship, so imagine what it will be like for those who read your research later. Add a relationship chart that indicates the relationship any time that you add someone new to any of your files so that the family relation is clear and easy to figure out.

Any genealogy website will provide you with relationship charts, and they are very easy to use. At the top of the chart, as well as on the left side, write child, grandchild, great grandchild, and so on. This represents the simplest relationships. As we move to the middle of the chart, things become a little more confusing.

In the first column from the top, write "brother or sister," "niece or nephew," "grandniece or grandnephew," and "great-grandniece or great-grandnephew".

The second column should contain "niece or nephew," "first cousin," "1st cousin, once removed," and "first cousin, twice removed".

In the third column, add "grandnephew or niece," "first cousin, once removed," "second cousin," and "second cousin, once removed".

In the fourth column, add "great-grandnephew or niece," "first cousin, twice removed," "second cousin, once removed," and "third cousin".

This is a standard relationship chart. It is and will always be difficult to read for those who have no experience, but the chart shows relationships that go so far back that they represent people the current generation may never have heard of. The chart is useful for you, the writer. It makes things a little clearer for you, but may be slightly confusing to a newbie.

During your research, you may discover that you have siblings from one family who married siblings from another family. This relationship is categorized as "double-cousins". For example: your grandfather and his brother married your grandmother and her sister.

When you read registers or newspapers, you may find some terms you haven't heard before. Some names of the relationships between siblings have changed over time. In order to avoid missing a relative or misclassifying one, find a family term glossary online or in a library.

Collect All Possible Information

What begins as a curiosity quickly becomes a hobby, and sometimes even an obsession in the long run. You may find yourself enjoying those long hours looking for one single fact. How can you know where to look? When you decide to create a genealogical tree, think about all of the information search options available today. There are plenty to choose from and learn from, each with unique pros and cons. At the end of your search, you will be happy to discover that you have learned more about your family than you expected when you started the project.

Learn About Your Options

When you begin the research, the first logical thing to do is go to your parents, grandparents, aunts and uncles, or even someone younger who has started doing the same research. You'll hear stories about them and about older siblings. The time passes pleasantly when family surrounds you.

The first thing to ask is their names, especially maiden names, because those are more difficult to track. If you know that your family lived in another city, state, or country at one time, ask where they grew up or were born. If a member was born in another country and then brought to America, ask if there are any siblings left in the old country. Ask a lot of questions to make your research efforts far more fruitful. You may still wind up with a few dead ends, but it can save you far more trouble than it will cause in most cases.

Interviewing your family member is fun and won't seem like work, but you can't limit your research to family interviews or memories. Other options should be explored. Over the last few decades since genealogy has become popular, hundreds of databases have appeared online. People from the same family often do family research without knowing it, even distant relatives. Seek the help of a professional if you are able to pay money for their often-flawless services, which usually are guaranteed. Because the pros have access to more options than the average Joe or Jane, they usually offer more than you can find on your own as an amateur.

However, most of us do the research ourselves, and there are many databases you can use. You can find services online that guarantee results for even the most ancient family members, within reason. Family will be your greatest asset though, especially the family elders.

The Internet Is Your Friend

Interviewing your family members will not get the job done. You must go further and do more research. Family members will only be able to tell you a limited amount of information, because they may not know more, or some may be ashamed of their history. It is up to you to document more and create a solid genealogical tree, noting even those ignominious, ill fated, or infamous family members.

Most of us know that the Internet grants access to almost any information. You may think that genealogy is not a very well documented area, but there are plenty of websites that provide information 24/7. All you need is a device such as a computer (or smartphone) and an Internet connection. Don't limit yourself to stories you hear from the family, go deeper. You have a chance to learn so much about your family's history that you should not pass up the chance to use search programs to find exactly what you need.

Try some of these tips for search ideas:

• Religious organizations. Family members are part of many different religious organizations, each with their own records. This may include Protestant churches, Jewish synagogues, mosques, LDS records, tribal documents, and much more.

• Chat room and online forums. A forum is a virtual room where people all over the world gather and discuss information on a specific subject. You may find blogs from those who have written genealogical information for your family. Consider starting your own blog to help others.

Ask Others to Give You a Hand

While the family can be a great help in your research endeavors, do not be afraid to seek some professional help when you come to the end of your rope. There may be websites that you cannot navigate or do not understand, or you may reach a point where you've exhausted all of the methods you know but are still lacking information. Professionals are usually worth what you pay, but you have to find someone reputable and reliable to avoid a long wait with no results.

Which professionals offer the best services?

You will find many professionals online, many of which will use e-mail as a primary method of communication. There are many professionals, but that doesn't mean they all offer quality services. It's smart to work with bigger companies, not individuals, because they often offer the best and largest databases. Consider the following advice before choosing a professional research company:

- How long has the professional worked in the genealogy business? Those who are just getting started may not charge as much, but this is not always a positive things. It may indicate that they have little or no experience. Lower prices are their weapons. You should aim for those professionals who have a few years of experience. Ask for references to make sure that they are not lying. Also, ask about the highest number of generations they have ever tracked for a family.

- What is the game plan for a family project such as yours? Professional genealogists should be able to offer you information about how they plan to deal with your situation, including what resources they are going to use. This should include war histories, church histories, vital statistics, ship registries, etc. They should have many options. The more they have, the more accurate the result will be for your project.

- How much will they charge for your project? There are genealogists who overcharge you and there are genealogists who ask for a lower rate than they should. Compare all of them and choose those whose rates suit your needs, not too high, but not too low or they may add additional fees later.